CONTINENTS

Africa

Leila Merrell Foster

Heinemann Library
Chicago, Illinois

© 2001 Reed Educational & Professional Publishing
Published by Heinemann Library,
an imprint of Reed Educational & Professional Publishing,
Chicago, IL

Customer Service 888-454-2279

Visit our website at www.heinemannlibrary.com

Designed by Depke Design
Printed in Hong Kong

05 04 03 02 01
10 9 8 7 6 5 4 3 2 1

Library of Congress Cataloging-in-Publication Data
Foster, Leila Merrell.
     Africa / Leila Merrell Foster.
          p. cm. -- (Continents)
     Includes bibliographical references (p.) and index.
     ISBN 1-57572-446-4
     1. Africa--Juvenile literature. [1. Africa.] I. Title. II. Continents (Chicago, Ill.)

DT3 .F67 2001
960--dc21

                                       00-011464

Acknowledgments
The publishers are grateful to the following for permission to reproduce copyright material:
Bruce Coleman, Inc./M.P. Kahl, p. 5; Earth Scenes/Frank Krahmer, p. 7; Tony Stone/Nicholas Parfitt, p.9; Tony Stone/Jeremy Walker, p.11; Bruce Coleman Inc./Brian Miller, p. 13; Animals Animals/Bruce Davidson, p. 14; Bruce Coleman, Inc./Nicholas DeVore III, p. 15; Earth Scenes/Zig Leszczynski, p. 16; Bruce Coleman, Inc./Lee Lyon, p. 17; Corbis/Arthur Thevena, p. 19; Corbis/AFP, p. 20; Bruce Coleman, Inc./Bob Burch, p. 21; Corbis/K.M. Westermann, p. 22; Photo Edit/Paul Conklin, p. 24; Bruce Coleman, Inc/John Shaw, p. 25; Tony Stone/Sylrain Grandadam, p. 26; Bruce Coleman, Inc./Norman Myers, p. 27; Animals Animals/Leen Van der Silk, p. 28.

Some words are shown in bold, **like this.**
You can find out what they mean by looking in the glossary.

Contents

Where Is Africa?

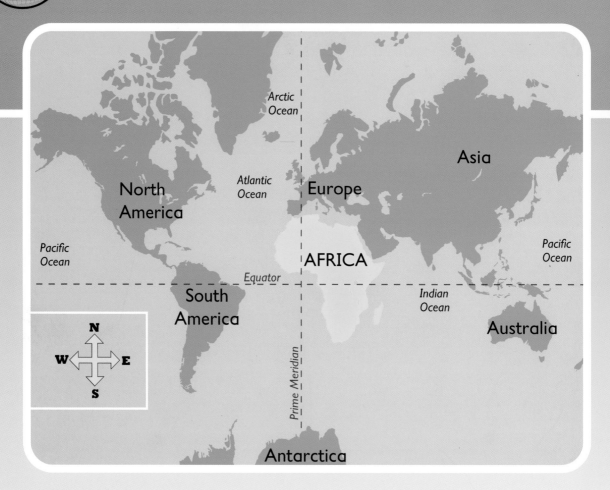

Arctic
Ocean

Asia

North
America

Atlantic
Ocean

Europe

Pacific
Ocean

Pacific
Ocean

AFRICA

Equator

South
America

Indian
Ocean

N

Australia

W E

S

Prime Meridian

Antarctica

There are seven continents in the world. Africa is the second largest. It is split in half by the **equator.** The **prime meridian** crosses it from north to south.

Cape Town, South Africa

Like most continents, Africa is surrounded by water. The Atlantic Ocean is to the west and the Indian Ocean is to the east. The Mediterranean Sea is to the north.

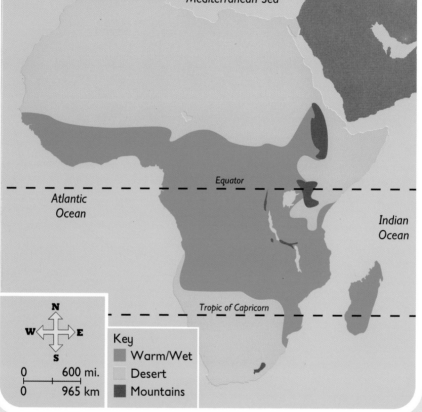

Mediterranean Sea

Equator

Atlantic
Ocean

Indian
Ocean

Tropic of Capricorn

N
W E
S

0   600 mi.
0   965 km

Key
Warm/Wet
Desert
Mountains

Because Africa sits on the **equator,** it gets very hot.
In the middle and the west are wet jungles. The
jungles get heavy rain and are usually very **humid.**

Namib Desert, Namibia

Huge deserts cover large parts of the north and south. The temperatures are very hot and little rain falls. High in the mountains it is cold and snowy.

Mountains and Deserts

Mount Kilimanjaro, Tanzania, Kenya

Mount Kilimanjaro is the tallest mountain in Africa. It is on the **border** of Tanzania and Kenya. The Drakensberg Mountains are in the south. The Atlas Mountains are in the north.

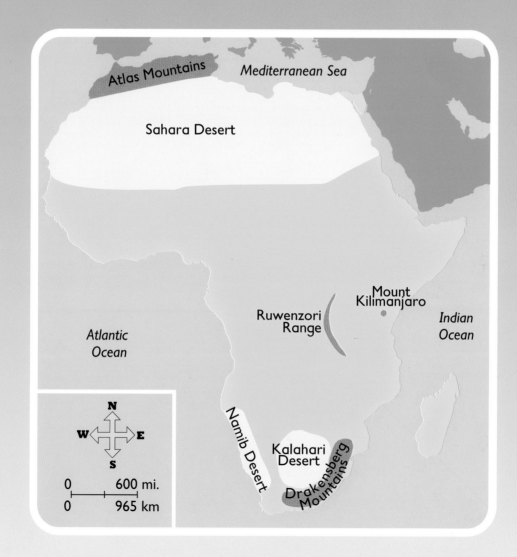

The Sahara Desert in the north is one of the largest deserts in the world. Temperatures get very hot. The Namib and Kalahari are other deserts in Africa.

Rivers

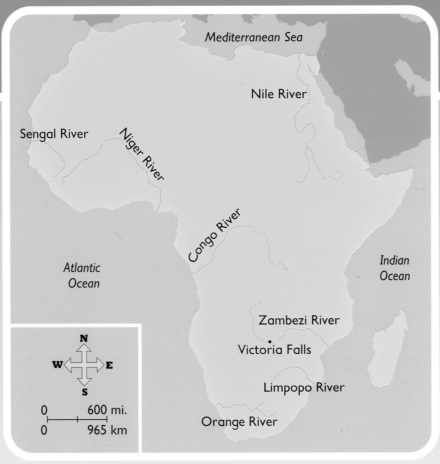

Mediterranean Sea

Nile River

Sengal River

Niger River

Congo River

Atlantic
Ocean

Indian
Ocean

Zambezi River

Victoria Falls

Limpopo River

Orange River

N
W E
S

| 0 | 600 mi. |
| 0 | 965 km |

The Nile and the Congo are the most important
rivers in Africa. The Nile is the longest river in the
world. It flows north to the Mediterranean Sea.

Victoria Falls, Zimbabwe

Victoria Falls is a waterfall on the Zambezi
River. It is called the "smoke that thunders"
because of the noise and water spray made from
the falling water.

Lakes

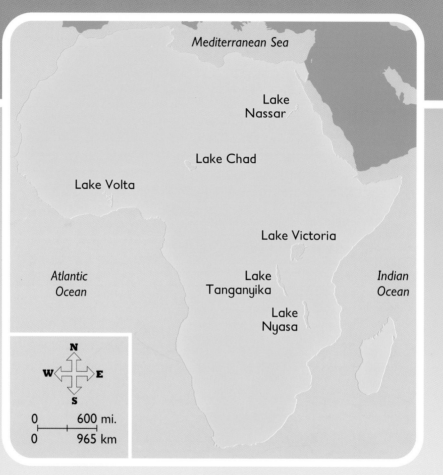

Mediterranean Sea

Lake Nassar

Lake Chad

Lake Volta

Lake Victoria

Atlantic Ocean

Lake Tanganyika

Indian Ocean

Lake Nyasa

N
W E
S

0   600 mi.
0   965 km

Africa has many lakes along its rivers. Some are **natural lakes**. Others were made when people built **dams** on rivers.

Lake Victoria, Uganda

Lake Victoria is one of the world's largest **freshwater** lakes. It has more than 200 kinds of fish. Many people live along its **shores.**

Animals

Elephants, Kenya

Africa has many wild animals. Groups of elephants, rhinoceroses, giraffes, lions, and zebras live on grasslands called **savannas.**

Gorilla, Rwanda

Many animals live in special parks where they are safe. Scientists study gorillas and chimpanzees to learn how they live. The scientists try to protect the animals from hunters and other dangers.

Ebony wood art

Many kinds of trees and plants grow in the forests of Africa. Ebony is a hard, heavy, dark wood. People use it to make furniture and **sculptures.**

Papyrus plants, Nile River

Papyrus is a plant that grows in the **delta** of the Nile River. In **ancient** times, papyrus was cut and pressed together to make paper.

Languages

There are 53 countries in Africa. Many countries have their own languages. More languages are spoken in Africa than on any other continent.

Arab Market, Egypt

Many people in the north speak the Arabic language. In the south, many languages are spoken. Most of these are from the Khoisan or Bantu languages.

Lagos, Nigeria

Lagos is one of the largest cities in Africa. It has a **port** on the Atlantic Ocean. It is an important city for business.

Cairo, Egypt

Cairo, in the north, is a large city on the Nile
River. Cairo has many museums and schools.
People from all over the world come to see
the **ancient ruins.**

Casablanca, Morocco

Casablanca has one of the busiest **ports** in Africa. It is on the Atlantic Ocean in the north. It has many modern buildings and one of the world's largest **mosques**.

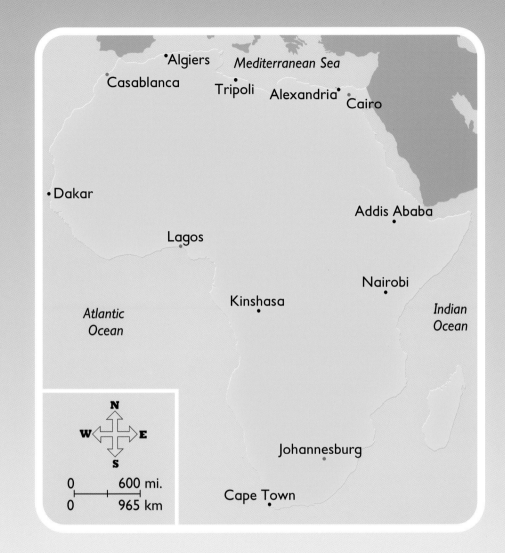

Algiers

Casablanca

Mediterranean Sea

Tripoli

Alexandria

Cairo

Dakar

Addis Ababa

Lagos

Nairobi

Kinshasa

Atlantic Ocean

Indian Ocean

Johannesburg

Cape Town

N
W E
S

| 0 | 600 mi. |
| 0 | 965 km |

Johannesburg is an important business center in the south. It was built in 1886 after gold was found nearby.

⊕ In the Country

Village in Guinea

Most people in Africa live in small villages. The
people in the villages have strong ties to their
families or **tribes.**

Herding cattle, Kenya

Many Africans raise **cattle.** These people must move from place to place to find food and water for their animals. Many of these people move to cities to get different jobs.

Pyramids of Giza, Egypt

The Great Pyramid of Giza is in Egypt. It was built about 4,500 years ago. The pyramid is a huge **tomb** for one of **ancient** Egypt's leaders.

Great Zimbabwe, Zimbabwe

Great Zimbabwe was an important stone city. It was built about 1,000 years ago. Today, the **ruins** are spread over many hills.

Zebras in Kruger National Park, South Africa

Kruger National Park is a place where wild animals are protected. The park has more kinds of animals than most other parks in Africa.

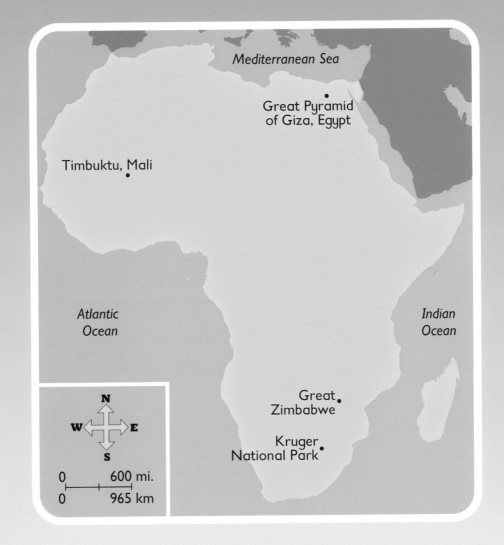

Mediterranean Sea

Great Pyramid
of Giza, Egypt

Timbuktu, Mali

Atlantic
Ocean

Indian
Ocean

N
W — E
S

0   600 mi.
0   965 km

Great
Zimbabwe

Kruger
National Park

Timbuktu was an **ancient trading** center near the Niger River. It was a place for **Muslim** teachers to meet. Salt dug out of the Sahara Desert is still brought by camels to this place.

Fast Facts

1. The Sahara Desert is almost as large as the United States.

2. The Nile is the world's longest river. It is 4,000 miles (6,400 kilometers) long.

3. There are more than 808 languages spoken in Africa.

4. Cairo is the largest city in Africa. It has about six million people.

5. Lake Tanganyika is 420 miles (680 kilometers) long. It is the longest freshwater lake in world.

6. The highest temperature ever recorded in the world was 136°F (58°C) in the shade at Al Aziziyah, Libya, on September 13, 1922.

Glossary

ancient something from a very long time ago

border line that divides one country or state from another

cattle farm animals, such as cows, bulls, steers, and oxen

dam barrier to hold back water

delta mouth of a river

equator imaginary circle around the exact middle of the earth

freshwater water that is not salty

humid wet or containing water

mosque building used for worship by Muslims

Muslim person who follows the Islam religion

natural lake lake that has not been made by people

port place where ships load and unload cargo

prime meridian most important imaginary north-south line that passes through Greenwich, England, and both the North and South Poles

ruin remains of something destroyed

savanna grassland containing scattered trees

sculpture art of carving or shaping wood, stone, clay, or metal into statues or other objects

shore land next to a body of water

tomb house or burial chamber for the dead

trading exchanging one thing for another

tribe group of people or families living together with the same leader or chief

More Books to Read

Dietz, James. Illustrated by Robert Cremmins. *Africa's Animal Giants.* Washington, D.C.: National Geographic Society, 1997.

Petersen, David. *Africa.* Danbury, Conn.: Children's Press, 1998.

Sammis, Fran. *Africa.* Tarrytown, N.Y.: Marshall Cavendish Corp., 1998.

Index